STARTING OUT

baby PUPPIES

LAURA K. MURRAY

CREATIVE EDUCATION • CREATIVE PAPERBACKS

CONT

ENTS

I AM A PUPPY.

I am a baby dog.

Look at
my ears!

At birth, my eyes are closed. My mother feeds me milk. I sleep most of the day for the first few weeks.

I have fur at birth. You can pet me softly.

Soon I can eat puppy food.

My first wobbly steps let me explore. I growl and play. My tail wags.

I keep learning!

I lose my puppy teeth.

I chew on everything! I am trained to sit, stay, and follow rules. Baths keep me clean. I get brushed and groomed.

I'll be your best friend!

SPEAK AND LISTEN

RRRRRUFF!

Can you speak like a puppy?

Dogs can bark, yip, growl, and whine.

Listen to these sounds:

Now it is your turn!

PUPPY WORDS

fur: the hairy coat of an animal

groom: to take care of a pet's coat, nails, and teeth

train: to teach a pet how to act

READING CORNER

Anderhagen, Anna. *Puppies: A First Look*. Minneapolis: Lerner, 2025.

Greenwood, Nancy. *My Pet Dog*. New York: Gareth Stevens, 2023.

Rossiter, Brienna. *My Pet Dog*. Mendota Heights, Minn.: Little Blue House, 2022.

INDEX

PUBLISHED BY CREATIVE EDUCATION AND CREATIVE PAPERBACKS
P.O. Box 227, Mankato, Minnesota 56002
Creative Education and Creative Paperbacks are imprints of The Creative Company
www.thecreativecompany.us

LIBRARY OF CONGRESS CATALOGING-IN-PUBLICATION DATA
Names: Murray, Laura K., 1989- author
Title: Baby puppies / Laura K. Murray.
Description: Mankato, Minnesota : Creative Education and Creative Paperbacks, [2026] | Series: Starting out | Includes bibliographical references and index. | Audience: Ages 4-7 | Audience: Grades K-1 | Summary: "Introduce beginning readers to the world of baby puppies with this life science starter. Includes photos, a labeled animal diagram, "Speak and Listen" section, glossary, and further resources"— Provided by publisher.
Identifiers: LCCN 2025015259 (print) | LCCN 2025015260 (ebook) | ISBN 9798895810354 library binding | ISBN 9781682779880 paperback | ISBN 9798895811610 ebook
Subjects: LCSH: Puppies—Juvenile literature
Classification: LCC SF426.5 .M865 2026 (print) | LCC SF426.5 (ebook) | DDC 636.7/07—dc23/eng/20250623
LC record available at https://lccn.loc.gov/2025015259
LC ebook record available at https://lccn.loc.gov/2025015260

DESIGN AND PRODUCTION
Design by Rhea Magaro
Art direction by Graham Morgan

PHOTOGRAPHS BY
Dreamstime/Anatoly Tiplyashin, 4, Benstacey80, 10, Isselee, 8, 11, 12, Michael Pettigrew, 5; Getty Images/francesco, 2, Gandee Vasan, 6, IzaLysonArts / 500px, 7; Pexels/Torsten Dettlaff, 14; Shutterstock/Viorel Sima, cover; Unsplash/Jametlene Reskp, 9

Printed in the United States